The Big Happy Vintage Easter Coloring Book

50+ Fun Coloring Pages of Vintage l
Eggs, Bunnies, Flowers, Baskets (For Teen and Adult Relaxation)

Ada Ashley

©LeVintagePrintage

In this coloring book, you will find charming illustrations of vintage Easter from master illustrators of the past, reproduced true to original in light grayscale, perfect for realistic coloring and art therapy relaxation.

The advantage of grayscale coloring over regular coloring is that the shading is already done, providing the depth and dimension to the final result. It also allows you using the existing shadows for guidance. General rule for grayscale coloring is simply to apply light colors over light gray areas, medium colors over medium gray areas and dark colors over dark gray areas. Alternatively you can start lightly with one color over larger areas and gradually add darker layers on top of it if you want more shading.

Illustrations are reproduced without hard outlines for the opportunity to color them as actual artwork and be proud to cut out and display after finishing. In addition to coloring, this book allows you to practice drawing, shading, and tracing based on the artwork of master illustrators. Coloring sheets are one-sided and blank on the back so they can be cut out for display or separate coloring.

Happy Easter!

AN EASTER TOKEN OF MY LOVE.

EASTER SOUVENIR.

Easter Greeting

EASTER FLOWERS.

Made in the USA
Middletown, DE
21 March 2021